Little Lamb

Learns about the Good Shepherd

Written and Illustrated

By

Jan Inman

ISBN: 1545127204
ISBN-13: 9781545127209

DEDICATION

For my Granddaughter Elliana

May you always love the Good Shepherd and His Word

Love you Little One, Mimmi

.

ACKNOWLEDGMENTS

I could not have done this without my amazing geeky husband, Jay

Thank-you for all your help and encouragement

I love you!

Mama and I were in the big, lush, green meadow where we spent most of our time.

We both loved the warm sunshine, the cool green grass and the brilliant blue sky that seemed to go on forever.

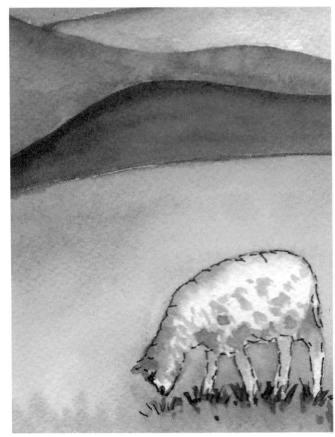

I felt safe here.

I was with my mama.

"Mama," I asked one day as I was always asking questions.

"Yes, little one?"

"Who is that man with the big stick?"

"Oh, He is the Good Shepherd," mama replied with a peaceful tone in her voice.

"He takes good care of us every day."

"He guides us and leads us in green pastures so we have everything we need. "

"*The Lord is my Shepherd, I shall not want.*

He makes me lie down in green pastures;

He leads me beside quiet waters."

"Mama?"

"Yes little one," mama gently replied.

"What are the sticks in his hands for?"

"One is for driving off animals that would hurt us, called a rod. The other is called a staff."

"One time when I was little, I was grazing on the tender grass and didn't see the water's edge. Suddenly, I was drowning in the stream. The Good Shepherd reached in with the crook of his staff and pulled me out. He is always watching over us and keeping us on the right path. I knew at that moment that the Good Shepherd would be with me even when I was scared."

"He restores my soul; He leads me in paths of righteousness for His name's sake.

Yes though I walk through the valley of the shadow of death, I will fear no evil, for You are with me; Your rod and your staff they comfort me."

"Mama?"

"Yes, little one," mama answered softly.

"Why does He put that stuff on our heads?"

Mama smiled as she replied, "Oh that is the oil He uses to keep flies away from our eyes and to heal our boo boos."

"You prepare a table before me in the presence of my enemies. You anoint my head with oil; my cup overflows."

"Mama?"

"Yes, little one," Mama braced herself to answer another question.

"I love the Good Shepherd. I want to follow Him all the days of my life and live where He lives."

A big smile came across Mama's face. "Yes, little one. So do I. I love Him too. "

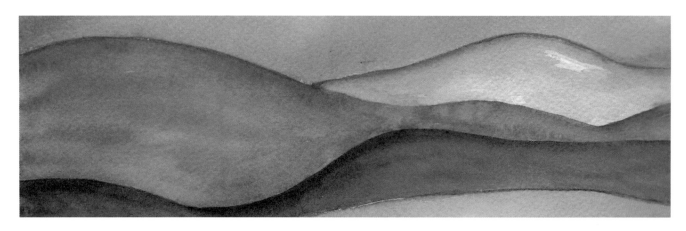

"Surely goodness and mercy shall follow me all the days of my life and I will dwell in the house of the Lord forever."

~Psalms 23~

The LORD is my Shepherd, I shall not want.

He makes me lie down in green pastures,

He leads me beside quiet waters, He restores my soul.

He guides me in paths of righteousness

for His name's sake.

Even though I walk through the valley

of the shadow of death,

I will fear no evil, for You are with me;

Your rod and Your staff, they comfort me.

You prepare a table before me in the

presence of my enemies.

You anoint my head with oil; my cup overflows.

Surely goodness and mercy will follow me

all the days of my life,

And I will dwell in the house of the LORD forever.

Amen.

Journal: Special memories with your Little One

_____

_____

_____

_____

_____

_____

_____

_____

_____

ABOUT THE AUTHOR

Jan is a Texas girl loving life in Colorado with her wonderful husband Jay. She is a proud momma of four amazing children and one very special granddaughter. She loves God's word and has always wanted to write and illustrate a children's book. This is hopefully the first of many!

Made in the USA
Middletown, DE
30 October 2021